W9-CJS-416

"Each second we live is a new and unique moment of the universe, a moment that will never be again... And what do we teach our children? We teach them that two and two make four and that Paris is the capital of France.

When will we also teach them: do you know who you are? You are a marvel. You are unique. In all the years that have passed, there has never been another child like you. And look at your body – what a wonder it is! Your legs, your arms, your clever fingers, the way you move. You may become a Shakespeare, a Michelangelo, a Beethoven. You have the capacity for anything. Yes, you are a marvel. And when you grow up, can you then harm another who is, like you, a marvel? You must cherish one another. You must work – we must all work – to make this world worthy of its children."

Pablo Casals

A famous Spanish musician, also noted for his humanitarian beliefs.

(1876-1973)

I'm Hip-hop, the rapping rabbit from a starship far away,

It looks so good down here on Earth, I think I'm going to stay.

I just love this planet and you human beings too,

And I've bounced across five galaxies to have a word with you...

LIFE EDUCATION

My Wonderful Body

Written by
Alexandra Parsons

Illustrated by
Ann Johns, John Shackell, Paul Banville, and Stuart Harrison

FRANKLIN WATTS

A Division of Grolier Publishing

LONDON • NEW YORK • HONG KONG • SYDNEY
DANBURY, CONNECTICUT

8944282

© Franklin Watts 1996
Text © Life Education/Franklin Watts

First American Edition 1997 by
Franklin Watts
A Division of Grolier Publishing
Sherman Turnpike
Danbury, Connecticut 06816

Parsons, Alexandra.
    My wonderful body / Alexandra Parsons.
      p. cm. -- (Life education)
    Includes index.
    Summary: A basic introduction to the human
body, describing its functions and how to care
for it.
    ISBN 0-531-14409-7
    1. Body, Human--Juvenile literature. [1. Body,
human.] I. Title. II. Series.
QM27. P276 1997
612--dc20   95-46358
                                        CIP AC

10 9 8 7 6 5 4 3 2 1

Edited by: Helen Lanz
Designed by: Sally Boothroyd
Commissioned photography by:
Peter Millard
Illustrations by: Ann Johns,
John Shackell, Paul Banville,
and Stuart Harrison
**Consultant for anatomical
illustrations:** Dr. Micheal Redfern

Printed in Italy

Acknowledgments:
Commissioned photography by Peter Millard:
5; 9; 10 (both); 12; 16; 21.
Researched photographs: Sally Boothroyd 7;
Bruce Coleman 15; Bubbles 11, 18.
Artwork: all cartoons of "alien" by Stuart
Harrison. Other cartoon illustrations by Ann
Johns: cover; title page; 7 (all); 8 (right); 9 (left); 13
(right middle); 17 (bottom right); 19 (center); 20
(all); 21 (all): John Shackell: contents page; 4 (all);
13 (left middle); 14 (all); 15 (all); 17 (center); 18.
Anatomical illustrations by Paul Banville: 5 (all); 6;
8 (left); 9 (top right); 10 (both); 12; 16.

Franklin Watts and Life Education International
are indebted to Vince Hatton and Laurie Noffs
for their invaluable help.

Franklin Watts would like to extend their special
thanks to all the actors who appear in the Life
Education books:

Calum Heath   Jade Hoffman
Frances Lander   Karamdeep Sandhar

Contents

My Outside . . . .

Your body is a wonderful piece of living machinery.
If you look after it properly, it will last you a lifetime.

INSTRUCTIONS ▶
Feed with interesting programs. Always follow the instructions. Don't use the keyboard with sticky fingers.

▲ INSTRUCTIONS
Feed with oil, gasoline, and water. Take to the mechanic if it goes wrong. Drive carefully.

Super skin facts

☺ *Every 50 days you get a new top layer of skin.*

☺ *Skin color depends on where your ancestors lived. Long, long ago, people who lived in sunny places developed dark skin to protect themselves from the burning rays of the sun. People who lived in cold countries had pale skin. Now many people's skin color is somewhere in between.*

◀ INSTRUCTIONS
Feed the body with fresh food, fresh air, and plenty of water. Feed the brain with plenty of interesting things. Take to the doctor if it gets sick. Give it lots of love and affection. Rest when tired. Exercise regularly.

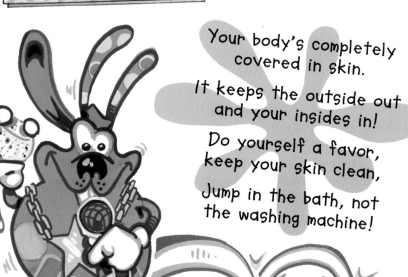

Your body's completely covered in skin.

It keeps the outside out and your insides in!

Do yourself a favor, keep your skin clean,

Jump in the bath, not the washing machine!

Look in the mirror and what do you see?

You've got a head, two bright eyes, a nose to smell, two ears to hear, a mouth for talking and eating, and a neck that joins your head to your chest.

You've got shoulders to join your arms to your body, two arms with elbows so they can bend.

Two wrists so your hands can move, two hands, eight fingers, and two thumbs.

You've got a chest, a waist, a tummy, and a bottom.

You've got two hips to join your legs to your body, two thighs, knees with kneecaps so your legs can bend, two calves, two ankles so your feet can move.

And finally, you've got two feet and ten toes.

What's a body made of?

It is made up of tiny units called cells that stick together. Different cells make up the different parts of your body, so blood cells make blood, bone cells make bone, nerve cells make nerves, and skin cells make skin.

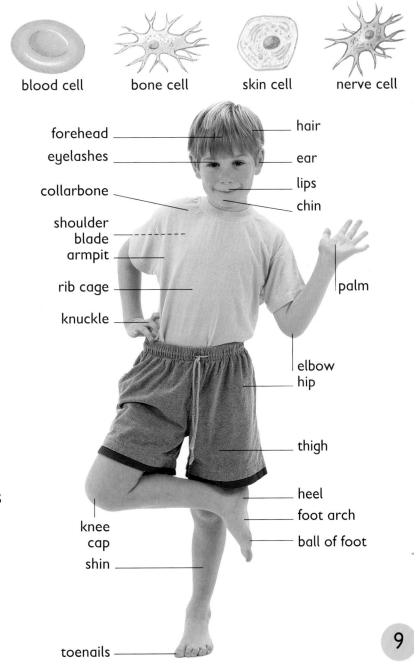

blood cell   bone cell   skin cell   nerve cell

forehead
eyelashes
collarbone
shoulder blade
armpit
rib cage
knuckle

hair
ear
lips
chin

palm
elbow
hip
thigh

knee cap
shin

heel
foot arch
ball of foot

toenails

9

My Bones . . . .

Your bones hold you up, give you your shape and protect your insides. Without bones, your body would be a big wobbly blob.

☆ Your skull protects your precious brain.

☆ Your spine is hollow! Inside the protective tunnel of your spine is a bundle of very important nerves, which carry messages from your brain to all parts of your body.

☆ Your ribcage protects your heart and lungs.

☆ Your breastbone holds your ribs together at the front. Your spine holds them at the back.

☆ Your hipbone is shaped like a bowl. It is actually made of eleven bones joined together.

☆ Your rib bones are thin and springy.

☆ Your arm and leg bones are long and thin.

☆ Over half of all the bones in your body are in your hands, wrists, feet, and ankles.

Bones keep your insides safe and sound.

Bones keep you upright, standing your ground.

Each bone is different, specially made,

From your little finger to your shoulder blade.

Bone up on some facts

☺ The smallest bone in the body is a little bone inside your ear. It is about the size of a pea.

☺ The biggest bone in anyone's body is the thigh bone.

☺ When fully grown, the human body has 206 bones. Each bone is different. They all have different jobs to do.

Broken bones

Your bones are strong, but light. Children's bones are growing all the time. If a bone gets broken, it will mend itself (as long as the bits have been put back in the right place!). Children's bones mend faster than grown-ups' bones.

Poor Jess broke her wrist. She wore her plaster cast for two weeks.

This giraffe has seven neck bones, the same number as you do. But, as you might expect, the giraffe's neck bones are quite a bit longer than yours.

Slugs have no bones at all, and neither do insects. Insects often have hard, shiny skin to protect their insides.

My Muscles . . . .

Your body wouldn't be much use to you if you couldn't move it. And that is why you've got muscles. Muscles are like thick rubber bands and they are everywhere! You've got tiny muscles in your eyelids so you can blink, and big strong muscles in your legs so you can run and jump.

Muscles in the body

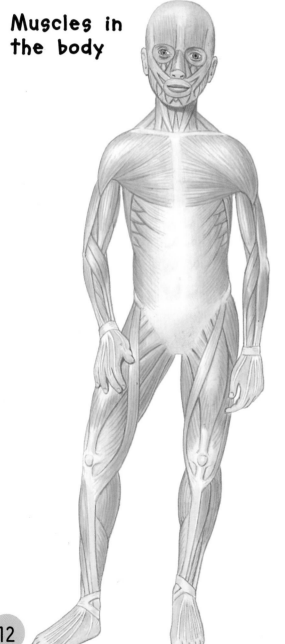

◄ Make a silly face! You are using your face muscles.

See how many movements you can make with your arms! You are using your arm, upper back, and upper chest muscles. ▶

◄ Pick up a pencil! You are using your hand and wrist muscles.

Take a deep breath! ▶ You are using the muscles between your ribs and your tummy muscles.

◄ Bend over! You are using your back and tummy muscles.

Some muscle facts

☺ Your smallest muscle is in your ear and your biggest is your thigh muscle.

☺ You use 17 muscles to smile and 43 to frown.

☺ You've got 656 muscles, so don't try to use them all at once!

◄ Jump up high! You are using your leg and foot muscles.

▲ Blink! You are using your eye muscles.

Talk! You are using your mouth and tongue muscles. ▶

How muscles work

Muscles can only pull — they can't push. So muscles work in pairs. When you bend your arm the top muscle pulls, and the bottom muscle stretches. Then when you straighten your arm, the bottom muscle pulls, and the top one stretches.

Muscle fuel

Muscles need energy so they can keep pulling and stretching for you. They get their energy from good, healthy food like vegetables, fruit, and protein. The more you exercise your muscles, the more they like it and the stronger they get.

Move that body, touch those toes,

Stamp that foot and wrinkle that nose.

Hear what I say, get mo–bil–ized,

Eat good food and ex–er–cise.

My Heart and Lungs . . . .

Cells in your body always need to repair and replace themselves. To do this they need two things: food and oxygen. Oxygen is a gas in the air we breathe. When we breathe in, thousands of tiny blood vessels in the lungs pick up the oxygen and take it into the blood stream. The heart then pumps the new supply of oxygen in the blood all around the body.

When you breathe in, your lungs fill with air. Lungs are made up of millions of tiny air sacs. Each sac is surrounded by lots of blood vessels. These take the oxygen from the air in the sac and pass it into the main blood stream. Breathe deep!

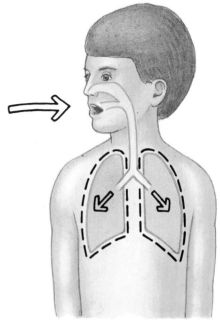

Your heart and lungs are safely tucked away inside your rib cage.

Your heart is a hard-working bundle of muscle about the size of a grown-up's fist. It pumps blood full of oxygen and other good things into blood vessels that are like a network all over the body. Blood that has given up all its oxygen comes back into the heart, and gets pumped around the lungs to get a fresh supply.

Hearts need exercise!

Your heart is made of a special kind of muscle that just keeps on beating without your ever having to think about it. (Isn't your body clever?) Like every other muscle in your body, heart muscle needs exercise to keep healthy. You can exercise your heart by moving around a bit every day, or cycling or skipping so your heart beats faster for a while. That's what a heart likes!

Here are some hearts and lungs having a really good time.

The air goes in and
goes round and round,
Pumped by the blood to
the heartbeat sound.
If a heart craves
some exercise,
We shouldn't hesitate
to oblige.

Remember this!

☺ You have got almost 62,000 miles of blood vessels snaking around inside your body.

☺ It takes about 20 seconds for a blood cell to travel all around the body.

☺ There are over 300 million air sacs in each lung. That's too many to count!

My Tummy . . . .

It is very important to eat the right kind of food, because eventually the food you eat becomes part of you! Let's see what happens to this juicy apple.

First stop is your mouth, where your teeth chew up the apple into pieces small enough to swallow.

Your food pipe is lined with special muscles to push the little pieces of apple down to your stomach.

Next stop is your tummy – your stomach. The stomach is like a bag of muscle with a lot of strong chemicals sloshing about inside it. The chemicals get to work on the apple, and the muscles in the stomach wall crush the apple to a pulp.

By the time your stomach has finished its job, your apple looks more like apple soup.

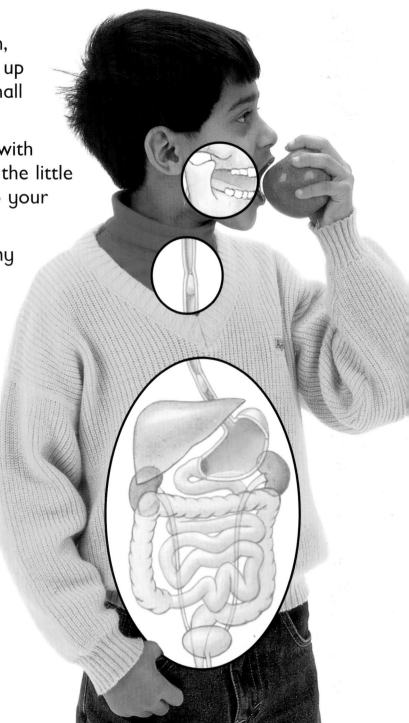

Next stop is the small intestine. This is a long, wiggly tube, about 20 feet long. Tiny blood vessels take in the nutrients, or goodness, the body can use, and pass them into the liver.

The liver sorts everything out. It sends good things into the blood stream to be delivered all around the body. This is to help repair worn-out cells and to build up your body and your brain. The liver works hard to change things that are not quite so good, like greasy foods and sweets, into something the body can use.

Your kidneys take liquid waste and water out of the blood stream. The liquid gets stored in your bladder. The waste that the body doesn't want continues on its journey into the large intestine. The walls of this larger but shorter tube – it is about 5 feet long – suck up the water, so the waste becomes solid. The liquid and solid waste come out when you go to the bathroom.

Hard to swallow!

☺ If our digestive systems were straight instead of curled up inside us, human beings would be almost 30 feet tall!

☺ Cows have four stomachs. They can suck up bits of chewed grass into their mouths from their stomach and chew it some more. When the grass has nothing left to chew, it goes on down into the cow's intestines.

Man, what a journey!
Boy, what a ride!
Fancy all that goin' on inside!
If my food's gonna end up as me,
I'll choose my meals more carefully!

17

My Senses . . . .

You have five senses to help you understand what is going on around you: hearing, sight, smell, taste, and touch. Special pathways, called nerves, run all over your body, something like telephone wires. Nerve endings in your ears, eyes, tongue, nose, and skin send information from the outside down the wires to the brain. The brain can then work out what is going on and what ought to be done about it.

BOOOOM!

Ear: Big loud booming noise – what do you think it is?

Brain: We've heard one of those before. It's thunder. I'll send a message to the legs to run home right away.

Eye: Oooh... it's got smiley parts and twinkly parts... I like it. I wonder what it is?

Brain: It's your Mom. I'll send a message to your mouth to give her a big smile.

Nose: It's got a hint of this and a bit of that...

Brain: It's your favorite – spaghetti. I'll send a message to your mouth to get ready for a treat.

Taste bud: Frankly brain, I don't like this at all. It's sort of bitter, and it's puckered me up...

Brain: Spit it out, you idiot! It's not ripe and it might give us a stomach ache!

Skin: I'm.... not enjoying this much. Ouch!

Brain: It's that scratchy sweater again... Just settle down, skin. You'll get used to it after a while.

Skin: Don't tell me what to do! You know how sensitive I am! I think I'll break out in a rash!

Your senses work hard just for you,

And they've got quite a lot to do.

It's their job to sort you out,

Tell you what the world's all about.

It's sensational!

☺ Cats have better sight than we do. Foxes have much better hearing, and dogs have a brilliant sense of smell.

☺ The muscles that make your eyes focus move about 100,000 times a day.

My Brain . . . .

Your brain is the cleverest thing about you. It is where your ideas and your feelings come from, where everything you have learned ends up and where your memories are stored. It isn't much to look at – it looks a little like a huge walnut. But that walnut is YOU!

Your brain is very delicate and is protected by your skull.

You're brilliant!

☺ The brain itself can feel no pain.

☺ The average brain contains 10,000 million brain cells. That's a lot!

☺ Messages travel within the brain at over 250 miles per hour. That's fast!

Your brain is your body's control.

It makes sure you know what to do.

So take good care of your brain.

And it will take care of you!

All parts of your brain have the job of sorting the messages sent from the five senses. Your brain is a huge store room holding everything you've ever learned and the memory of everything that has ever happened to you.

The right side of your brain controls the muscles of the left side of your body. It also works out how to put things together – a skill you need for both music and math!

Your brain is the boss! It controls everything that happens in the body. The back of the brain takes care of things you don't even think about, like breathing, coughing, sneezing, and digesting your dinner.

The left side of the brain makes it possible for you to speak, write and read. This control station also sends messages to the muscles on the right side of your body.

How does a brain keep going?

With your help! Brains need you to feed them well on healthy foods, give them plenty of sleep, and stay away from alcohol, cigarettes, and other drugs that mess up their control systems.

Thankyou!

My Self . . . .

We know that we've all got 206 bones, 656 muscles, zillions of brain cells, a heart and a stomach, and all the other parts that make up our bodies. So why aren't we all the same? Each one of us is unique because we are made up of a special combination of things we have inherited from our parents.

How babies grow

A baby grows inside its mother from a tiny egg. Inside the egg are all the special instructions that will make the baby grow up. These instructions are called genes. Half of the genes come from the mother and half from the father.

> Fair hair
> Freckles
> Good at math
> Big feet
> Love from MOM

> Brown eyes
> Long legs
> Going to get gray hair early (sorry)
> Good at telling jokes
> Love from Dad

Can you imagine what this little egg is going to look like, and what kind of a person she will be?

Brothers and sisters

Even brothers and sisters are different, because each one gets a different bundle of genes from their parents.

All the children got their father's hair. The eldest boy got his dad's mouth and his younger brother got his dad's sense of humor. The baby got her mother's calm nature.

The one and only!

So, you see, you are absolutely unique. There is no one else like you in the world! That makes you very special. You have got your inheritance, but now it is up to you to make something of it. Even if your parents are terribly healthy, you won't be unless you eat well and exercise. And even if your parents are terribly smart, you won't be unless you fill up your **own** brain with your **own** knowledge.

Your genes are yours and my genes are mine.

You will be you, and you will be fine.

You will be fine because now you know,

It's **you** that decides just how **you'll** grow.

Kids can make their own decisions about how they look after their bodies and their brains.

Gene genius

☺ *Some genes are stronger than others. Brown eye genes are stronger than blue eye genes.*

☺ *You inherit the way you look from your parents, but your personality depends a little on your genes and a lot on the way you live your life.*

My Life . . . .

Who's in charge of your life? You are! Think of all the things you can do to keep your body fit and active. You have only one body, and a healthy body is much more use to you than an unfit one. And don't forget that hardworking brain of yours. It needs to be fed with new ideas, friendship, love, and affection.

An unhappy body

A happy body

Oh, that feels good. A good boost of energy to start the day.

Aah! Nice bit of fresh air!

Just what we need, some exercise. Come on, one two, one two.

I'll store this information here, and a little there. So if 2+4=6, then 20+40=60! Got it!

2+4

Well, we've had quite a busy day. 2000+4000=6000! I'm ready for a rest.

Your body's an amazing living machine.

You've got to get into a good routine.

Look after your body as you should,

You'll look great and you'll feel good.

That's my message, man, take it or leave it!

LETTER FROM LIFE EDUCATION

Dear Friends:

The first Life Education Center was opened in Sydney, Australia, in 1979. Founded by the Rev. Ted Noffs, the Life Education program came about as a result of his many years of work with drug addicts and their families. Noffs realized that preventive education, beginning with children from the earliest possible age all the way into their teenage years, was the only long-term solution to drug abuse and other related social problems.

Life Education pioneered the use of technology in a "Classroom of the 21st Century," designed to show how drugs, including nicotine and alcohol, can destroy the delicate balance of human life. In every Life Education classroom, electronic displays show the major body systems, including the respiratory, nervous, digestive and immune systems. There is also a talking brain, a wondrous star ceiling, and Harold the Giraffe, Life Education's official mascot. Programs start in preschool and continue through high school.

Life Education also conducts parents' programs including violence prevention classes, and it has also begun to create interactive software for home and school computers.

There are Life Education Centers operating in seven countries (Thailand, the United States, the United Kingdom, New Zealand, Australia, Hong Kong, and New Guinea), and there is a Life Education home page on the Internet (the address is http://www.lec.org/).

If you would like to learn more about Life Education International contact us at one of the addresses listed below or, if you have a computer with a modem, you can write to Harold the Giraffe at Harold@lec.org and you'll find out that a giraffe can send E-mail!

Let's learn to live.

All of us at the Life Education Center.

Life Education, USA
149 Addison Ave
Elmhurst, Illinois
60126
USA
Tel: 630 530 8999
Fax: 630 530 7241

Life Education, UK
20 Long Lane
London
EC1A 9HL
United Kingdom
Tel: 0171 600 6969
Fax: 0171 600 6979

Life Education,
Australia
PO Box 1671
Potts Point
NSW 2011
Australia
Tel: 0061 2 358 2466
Fax: 0061 2 357 2569

Life Education,
New Zealand
126 The Terrace
PO Box 10-769
Wellington
New Zealand
Tel: 0064 4 472 9620
Fax: 0064 4 472 9609

Useful words

Air sacs Tiny compartments in your lungs that fill with air when you breathe in.

Blood stream The blood flowing within your body.

Blood vessels The long, thin tubes that your blood flows through. You have blood vessels going to every part of your body.

Cells Tiny units of living material that make up your body. There are millions and millions of cells in your body and different parts are made of different kinds of cells – you have blood cells, bone cells, brain cells, skin cells, and so on.

Energy The power to do work. Your body gets its energy from food, water, and oxygen.

Genes Genes are like messages inside cells. As a baby grows inside its mother, the genes tell the cells what features the baby will have – what color its eyes will be, how big its ears will be, and so on. Half your genes are from your mother and half from your father.

Nerves Tiny cells that carry messages around your body to and from your brain. There are special nerve pathways all over your body carrying information and sending messages to help you make sense of the world around you.

Nutrients The good things in food that your body uses to build itself up.

Oxygen A gas in the air that your body needs to live and grow. Oxygen is taken into your lungs when you breathe in and is carried through the blood stream all around your body.

Taste buds Tiny bumps on your tongue that pick up flavors and let your brain know what they are.

Index

28

Useful addresses

American Heart Association
7272 Greenville Avenue
Dallas, TX 75321
Telephone: 214-373-6300
Toll-free: 800-242-8721
Fax: 214-706-1341

American Lung Association
1740 Broadway
New York, NY 10019
Telephone: 212-315-8700
Fax 212-265-5642

President's Council on Physical
Fitness and Sports
701 Pennsylvania Avenue, NW
Suite 250
Washington, DC 20004
Telephone: 202-272-3421
Fax: 202-504-2064

TARGET
Helping Students Cope with
Tobacco, Alcohol, and Other
Drugs
11724 NW Plaza Circle
PO Box 20626
Kansas City, MO 64195
Telephone: 816-464-5400
Toll-free: 800-366-6667
Fax: 816-464-5571